Continually Transforming Koch Industries Through Virtuous Cycles of Mutual Benefit

By Charles G. Koch

I was introduced to hard work at an early age, including pitching hay when I was six.

Contents

We needed just two floors of a downtown office building to house a significant fraction of our 300 employees when I came here in 1961. Today, Koch Industries has 130,000 employees worldwide.

—

Founded on Principles

IN THIS SECTION

Koch's Framework for Success

Self-Actualization

Being Contribution Motivated

"The man who grasps principles can successfully select his own methods. The man who tries methods, ignoring principles, is sure to have trouble."

- HARRINGTON EMERSON

KOCH'S FRAMEWORK FOR SUCCESS

Over the past six decades, Koch Industries has transformed from a small family firm with a narrow focus into one of the largest privately held companies in America. Since 1960, we have entered dozens of new industries, added 130,000 employees and expanded into at least 60 countries — all while outperforming the S&P 500 by more than 30-to-1. We now make everything from popular consumer brands to industrial commodities and are well-established in the world of technology-driven change.

This booklet explains how and why Koch Industries has flourished and provides a guide for accomplishing much more. It illustrates how the focused application of the concepts and principles that make up Market-Based Management® (MBM®) transformed the entire trajectory of Koch Industries, helping us grow 7,000-fold. At its root, Market-Based Management is a framework designed to help organizations create virtuous cycles of mutual benefit, which we have accomplished by increasingly and more systematically applying MBM.

What is a virtuous cycle of mutual benefit? It is the process by which people and organizations continuously build capabilities that create value for others, a never-ending process that generates exponential growth. At Koch Industries, we have achieved five such cycles: in engineered solutions; in gathering, trading and distribution; in chemical process industries; in investments; and, most recently, in electronic and data technology. (We are not a conglomerate, as our capabilities are inter-related and mutually reinforcing.) We have grown tremendously in each area by creating goods and services that help others improve their lives. Insofar as Koch Industries has succeeded, it is because we have enabled others to succeed.

These mutually beneficial cycles were created by those who first created their own. They did so as the company increasingly focused on building a culture in which people could self-actualize. That is our goal for everyone here.

SELF-ACTUALIZATION & BEING CONTRIBUTION MOTIVATED

Self-actualization was defined by psychologist Abraham Maslow as realizing your potential — what he described as "everything one is capable of becoming." Achieving this requires discovering, developing and utilizing your innate abilities to live a life of meaning. Such people are contribution motivated, committed to helping others improve their lives, rather than being negatively motivated (like those who hoard knowledge or seek unfair advantages). When self-actualized people make a contribution to others and to society, it gives them such satisfaction that they strive to find further ways to contribute, leading to a lifetime of virtuous cycles. Self-actualized individuals willingly face reality, creatively solve problems and find fulfillment in helping others succeed.

Koch Industries' transformations have always depended on our employees' self-transformation, according to these principles. For the company to continue to

Psychologist Abraham Maslow stressed becoming "everything one is capable of."

create cycles of mutual benefit and succeed in this new world of rapid and fundamental change, we must continually improve our ability to enable our employees to transform themselves. Employees who do so not only enable the company to flourish — they realize their potential and have much more successful, fulfilling lives.

What you *can* be you *must* be.

Self-actualization can involve a course correction anytime in life, as it did for me. Despite earning three degrees in engineering, I was a lousy engineer, so I searched for another way to contribute. I found it by applying my conceptual aptitudes to learn the principles of scientific and social progress. I used these to develop a framework for business and life based on the principles of mutual benefit and continual transformation. I'm living proof that you can succeed beyond your wildest dreams by diligently developing your abilities and using them to create value for others. The same is true for people everywhere.

Although most of these pages focus on examples involving Koch Industries, my message is universal. Whether we're talking about an individual, an organization or a society, I am convinced that Maslow's observation was spot-on: What you *can* be, you *must* be.

Leaders at every level have an essential role in fostering a culture of self-actualization. Effective leaders not only live by our Guiding Principles (see Appendix), they regularly review them with employees and provide frequent and forthright feedback that stimulates dialogue and change. They hold themselves and their organizations accountable for applying these Principles in a way that enhances self-actualization, leading to virtuous cycles of mutual benefit.

While leaders are important in helping employees self-actualize, they cannot impose that kind of transformation. Virtuous cycles, whether individual or organizational, can only occur from the bottom up, as individuals develop and apply their abilities and as organizations do the same with their capabilities. To become self-actualized, employees must internalize our Guiding Principles through study and regular

Our expansion in the 1990s was dwarfed by the much greater transformations in the years that followed.

practice until they can apply them instinctively. Self-actualization is the last Principle because it only comes about by internalizing the other seven Principles: Integrity; Stewardship and Compliance; Principled Entrepreneurship™; Transformation; Knowledge; Humility; and Respect. All are necessary for success — yours, mine, the company's, and society's.

Koch Industries will continue to flourish only so long as you and I, as individuals, continually develop and improve ourselves. We must all become lifelong learners, committed to finding new ways to contribute. Fortunately, since everyone has a gift, we all are capable of meaningful

Newcomers to Koch, including college interns like these, have more opportunity than ever before.

contributions. With the right mindset and support, everyone can better themselves by bettering others. I hope these pages will help inspire you to become the best you can be.

We must all become lifelong learners, committed to finding new ways to contribute.

KEY REFLECTIONS

1. What is my unique gift? Am I developing and applying it?
2. Do I attempt to succeed by contributing or through negative behavior?
3. Am I internalizing and practicing all the MBM Guiding Principles?

To succeed long term, a business must become a preferred partner and undergo continual transformation.

Understanding Virtuous Cycles of Mutual Benefit

"If there is no transformation inside us, all the structural change in the world will have no impact on our institution."

- PETER BLOCK

EMPLOYEES' ROLE

To create virtuous cycles of mutual benefit, we need to understand their fundamentals and how each of us can contribute to them.

These cycles begin when we develop capabilities that enable us to create value for others. We apply these capabilities to serve the customers for whom we can create the most value and who will reward us accordingly. We call these cycles virtuous because they benefit all the parties involved, from yourself to society.

As we improve and apply our capabilities, new opportunities open, which point to the need for additional capabilities. This leads to never-ending cycles of improvement, growth, and contribution to others.

For an organization to create virtuous cycles, it must have employees who create their own internal virtuous cycles. In other words, employees who are self-actualizing. Such people discover their innate abilities, develop them into valued skills, apply them to maximize their contributions,

Self-actualized individuals continually learn, grow, and contribute at a higher level.

and then do it all over again. Individuals who follow this path — it is unique for each person — continually learn, grow, and contribute at a higher level, greatly increasing their ability to succeed, whatever their calling.

Employees translate their personal cycles into organizational virtuous cycles through two inter-related philosophies: becoming a **preferred partner** and **continual transformation**.

11

PREFERRED PARTNER

A preferred partner is someone who prefers working with you rather than their alternatives, because you do a superior job of providing what they value.

At Koch Industries, we strive to become the preferred partner, not only of customers but of all our constituencies: employees, suppliers, communities, co-investors, regulators, and society. To achieve this, we:

- Provide **customers** with products and services they value more than their alternatives. By anticipating what customers' alternatives will be, we can continue to create value for them in the future. Our preferred customers are those for whom we can create superior value who compensate us accordingly.

- Help **employees** realize their potential. This is why we select, develop, reward, and retain employees based on their commitment to our Guiding Principles. The primary role for every supervisor is to ensure that employees develop their innate abilities into valued skills, have roles for which they have a comparative advantage, and are rewarded for the value they create.

- Choose **suppliers** who share our vision and values, and can and will create the most value for us. Develop a relationship that enables them to create more value for us than their other customers and reward them accordingly.

- Locate in **communities** with the laws, culture, capabilities, and geographic location that enable us to create the most value. Be dedicated to making those communities a better place to live for everyone.

- Give preference to **investment partners** with aligned vision and values, and complementary capabilities. Strive to make the relationship mutually beneficial by helping them succeed.

- Understand what **regulators** are trying to achieve and then cooperate with them in a philosophy of mutual benefit. Encourage them to implement regulations in a way that helps rather than hinders people's ability to create value for others.

- Benefit **society** by practicing good stewardship and improving our ability to consume fewer resources, freeing those resources to satisfy other needs. Strive to remove barriers that prevent people from realizing their potential and urge others to do the same.

In short, we want people to be better off because of what we do and how we do it. When we create superior value for others (in whatever context), they choose to partner with us and enable us to build our capabilities and increase our contributions. Conversely, when we fail to provide superior benefits to our constituencies, they may look elsewhere, which limits our ability to generate virtuous cycles. Preferred partnerships are vital for progress.

CONTINUAL TRANSFORMATION

Similarly, continual transformation is always and everywhere a necessity. The alternative is extinction. Our attitude — as a business and as individuals — should be that however well we are doing, we can and must do much better at creating value for others. This is the only way to successfully deal with what Joseph Schumpeter described as creative destruction. "Businessmen," he said, are always "standing on ground crumbling beneath their feet."

Joseph Schumpeter emphasized the concept of Creative Destruction.

Given this reality, for an organization to succeed long term, it must have an effective vision — one that not only declares what it is trying to achieve, but provides a credible path toward that end. It must be realistic and based on the organization's capabilities. At Koch, our Vision is our North Star. It's not a destination. Rather, it is a constant guide and ever-present reminder of the path we believe best fits us.

The first paragraph of our Vision is as follows:

"The role of business in society is to help people improve their lives by providing products and services they value more highly than their alternatives, and do so responsibly while consuming fewer resources. To the extent a business accomplishes this, its profitability is a valid measure of the value it creates in society."

A beneficial, well-articulated vision motivates employees to be productive and innovative — but this will only happen if employees understand the particular vision that is relevant to their role, are committed to it, and are guided by appropriate measures. That is why we have made such an extensive effort to communicate KII's Vision, which each business and capability should use to create their own. An effective vision enables employees to be self-directed and to fully utilize their innate abilities.

Helping people improve their lives is fundamental to the role of business. To be successful long term, businesses must continually improve their products and services, and do so responsibly and efficiently, providing ever-greater benefits to every party involved. Only then will customers and others choose their offerings over the many available alternatives.

Successful businesses maximize the difference between the value they create for their customers and the value of those resources if consumed elsewhere. They also do their utmost to respect the rights of others.

This commitment is reflected in more than just the quality of their products and services. It requires creating a work environment in which the safety of employees and others is the highest priority, the environment is protected, laws and regulations are observed, and the temptation to corrupt the rules in hopes of profiting without creating value for others is resisted.

In our Vision, we stress the need to continually transform ourselves due to the reality of creative destruction. Although it threatens the very existence of long-standing jobs, firms, and industries, creative destruction also creates exceptional opportunities. To give us a better chance of capturing those opportunities, we need to fully understand this dynamic.

My own transformation resulted from focusing on my aptitudes and learning, and then applying abstract principles.

If the need to deal with creative destruction was important when Schumpeter wrote about it almost 80 years ago, it is exponentially more important today. Due to the ever-more-rapid pace of change, we have a heightened sense of urgency to transform our ability to create value and to use disruptive technologies when they will help us help others. All our people, businesses, and capabilities must become more aggressive in creating virtuous cycles of mutual benefit.

Our transformations are informed by knowledge networks within each business, throughout Koch, across our industries, and anywhere else that may be beneficial. These networks don't just happen, they are continually built. In keeping with our Republic of Science approach (see Section 7) we seek to understand trends anywhere in the world — from any and all useful sources — that might improve, disrupt, or destroy what we do today. To ignore such developments is organizational suicide.

FAILURES

Another important source of knowledge is experimentation. To generate widespread experimentation, we cultivate a culture of prudent risk taking without penalizing the failures that come from well-designed experiments. Successful experiments signal us to move forward. Unsuccessful ones tell us to change or stop, preventing much larger future losses. (Experimentation is just as, if not more, essential for individual self-actualization.)

The five presidents of KII (so far) after the company became Koch Industries: (L-R) Bill Hanna, Sterling Varner, Charles Koch, Joe Moeller, Dave Robertson.

Before undertaking any new venture or strategy, we need to demonstrate that we have the capabilities to create superior value. Do we understand all the factors that can cause it to fail? Are we capable of dealing with them? Like Karl Popper, we believe that the only "genuine test of a theory is the attempt to falsify it." This commitment to identifying the flaws prior to any undertaking is an essential aspect of our challenge process.

We are now more focused than ever on eliminating waste — anything that doesn't create value. This is why we relentlessly innovate to use fewer resources and minimize our environmental footprint. Over the last five years we have reduced our production-related waste by 16% and are recycling, recovering for energy or treating 92% of it. Our businesses have also reduced CO_2 emissions by nearly 10% during the past four years. Since 2013, we have implemented more than 1,200 pollution prevention activities, for which the Environmental Protection Agency has repeatedly named Koch the first- or second-ranked company for such initiatives. This reflects our commitment to mutual benefit: Using fewer resources and creating less waste is a win for us, the communities in which we operate, and society as a whole.

It is also wasteful to continue operating businesses when we are no longer able to create new virtuous cycles. This not only wastes our capital but the creative energy of our people, which is why we exit such businesses as soon as feasible.

As we transform our businesses, they become more labor efficient. This means fewer employees will be required for any given role and each role will be more demanding and fulfilling, but involve less drudgery and hazards. The good news, as history shows, is that this doesn't increase overall unemployment. That's because new jobs are created to produce the new products and services that replace the old. The hard part is learning the new skills that will enable you to continue to contribute. The only answer is to become a lifelong learner, which is a major reason we work so hard at helping our employees become self-actualized. A virtuous cycle will last only if we all continually learn, improve, and discover new opportunities to create value better than our competitors.

Many of our virtuous cycles have ended. Other investments that we hoped would become virtuous cycles never materialized. The causes are varied. Sometimes it's because of a failure of culture, a failure to continually innovate, superior innovation by others, or even outside influences beyond our control.

We relentlessly innovate to use fewer resources and minimize our environmental footprint.

A prime example of all these factors is the story of my father's thermal cracking process, which he developed in 1927. It helped independent refineries get higher yields, required less downtime and did not carry a royalty — all of which were major benefits to customers of Winkler-Koch Engineering. The business enjoyed a huge uptick when the process was introduced, selling 15 installations in just two years.

But the major oil companies, unhappy with this newfound competition from independent refiners, put an abrupt end to it by using their so-called Patent Club to sue Winkler-Koch and its customers. Although the Patent Club eventually lost every one of those cases (even after resorting to judicial bribery), the legal process took more than a decade, making it difficult for a virtuous cycle to start. My father's invention probably wouldn't have resulted in a virtuous cycle anyway, since no effort was being made to develop new capabilities and catalytic cracking would soon replace thermal cracking.

The process of creating virtuous cycles is seldom a journey of unmitigated successes. It is a trial-and-error process that results in setbacks and outright failures. Our ventures with chromatography systems, air quality consulting, dredge manufacturing, cryogenic systems, fiberglass pipe, and seawater desalination were all a bust. Their common denominator was our failure to properly apply the model of virtuous cycles of mutual benefit. Instead, we overestimated our capabilities, misjudged opportunities, were unable to become a preferred partner, or did not build suitable knowledge networks. As you will see time and time again on the following pages, we had to learn some difficult lessons the hard way — much as I have throughout my own life.

Creating virtuous cycles is seldom a journey of unmitigated successes.

One of the most painful lessons hit us in the late 1990s when our success led to hubris, degenerating into destructive spirals. We gave MBM lip service rather than truly applying it. We stopped hiring on values first and began believing we could succeed at anything, regardless of whether we had the capabilities needed to create value. And it got worse from there.

As is so often the case, these problems were rooted in our leadership, including me. I had been distracted by problems (including lawsuits) from several shareholders and needed help to get the company back on track. In 1999, I finally got my head clear enough to face the issues. My first step was persuading Joe Moeller to accept the role of president and COO.

Joe began dealing with the issues immediately, starting with the biggest: the serious deterioration of Koch Petroleum Group. Made up of the Pine Bend and Corpus Christi plants, as well as Koch Supply & Trading, KPG had long been an important contributor to Koch's earnings and ability to create virtuous cycles.

Everyone in our organization, regardless of role, is expected to learn and apply MBM to get results.

Joe wisely selected Dave Robertson as KPG's new leader. Dave had previously led its sales group and was known and trusted by long-time employees. His approach was to interview the KPG employees he felt would tell him the truth.

Those interviews revealed significant problems in all five dimensions of MBM:

Vision — The group had stopped focusing on creating value for customers. Instead, it was engaged in financial fakery and organizational manipulation.

Virtue and Talents — The senior leaders were not contribution motivated. They consistently violated our Guiding Principles. Meanwhile, good, long-term employees were being pushed out.

Knowledge Systems — Financial statements had become so complicated that they weren't useful in guiding decisions. Business activities were divided into profit centers which competed for credit and did not share knowledge. Challenge was punished rather than rewarded.

Decision Rights — The organization's structure and authorities were so confusing that decisions took a long time or weren't made at all.

Incentives — The scorecards for each group were rigged to show that it was performing well and should be rewarded, even though it was not. Actual profitability was a fraction of the value represented.

Based on these findings, the people causing the problems were quickly terminated and the organizational structure was simplified, with clear accountability and decision rights. The bogus scorecards were eliminated, and the financial statements began reflecting reality. We made it clear that employees would only be rewarded if they created real value for our customers and the company — if they pursued self-actualization, not stagnation.

Following these essential changes, performance quickly rebounded and KPG's profitability greatly improved. Instead of a destructive downward spiral, KPG began contributing to a virtuous cycle.

As Dave Robertson put it, "Individuals working in the business both identified all the problems and came up with all the solutions. The fix was a bottom-up approach recommended and implemented by team members committed to our MBM philosophy."

KEY REFLECTIONS

1. Am I helping us become the preferred partner of our constituencies?

2. Am I looking for opportunities to improve my performance through continual transformation? Or am I content doing what I've always done?

3. How can I better understand and apply the five dimensions and Guiding Principles of MBM to spur my own self-actualization?

Koch Engineering in the early 1960s lacked all the elements of virtuous cycles.

KOCH FLEXITRAY and

give higher capacities and efficiencies .

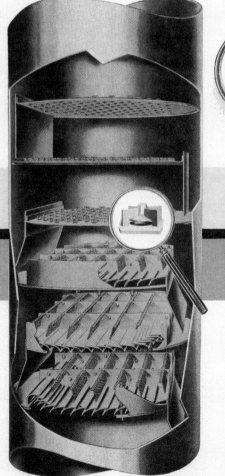

The "Flexitray," with its extreme flexibility and capacities approaching those of the best-designed perforated tray, has become an extremely popular addition to the Koch tray line. Complete success of this low-priced tray in more than 300 installations has resulted in its adoption by major companies for all services.

The dependable lift of graded weights of caps with increased vapor loads insure distribution at low loads, and provide a wide range of efficient operation without liquid runback.

The "FLEXITRAY" for high capacity and extreme flexibility

The "BENTURI" TRAY for extremely high capacity and lowest pressure drop

The Koch "Benturi"-type tray gives the minimum pressure drop per theoretical tray. The vapor riser is in the shape of a bent venturi, or "Benturi," and approaches the characteristics of a venturi within a plus or minus 2%. The kinetic energy of the vapors can obviously be most efficiently built up by a venturi. Further, the recovery of such energy is accomplished in agitation of the liquid and moving through the vertical perforated baffles has been proved by other Koch designs to be an excellent means of obtaining increased fractionating efficiency.

Over 600 installations have proved Koch's superiority over other devices in capacity, efficiency, flexibility, and lower pressure drop.

———

From Distillation Trays to Engineered Solutions

"You will never change things by fighting the existing reality. To change something, build a new model that makes the existing model obsolete."

– BUCKMINSTER FULLER

OUR FIRST VIRTUOUS CYCLE

In 1961, the year I returned to Wichita, we had just two businesses of note: Rock Island Oil & Refining and Koch Engineering. RI owned a crude oil gathering system in southwest Oklahoma that transported about 60,000 barrels of oil a day to a nearby main line. KE, based in Wichita, made internals (called trays) for distillation towers at refineries and chemical plants. I had worked summer jobs for both businesses as a teenager.

THE PERILS OF PROTECTIONISM

When I was given responsibility for KE, I soon realized it was short-sighted, protectionist, difficult to deal with, and more than willing to keep doing the same things the same old way. As a result, it failed to build capabilities that create value for others.

Most customers bought our products because they didn't have a better option, not because they were thrilled with us. We were no one's preferred partner and sorely lacking in transformation of any kind. This situation came about largely due to my father's health.

He was suffering from hypertension and heart ailments which left him with little strength and energy for office work, let alone building an effective management team. And although he was, in most ways, a tough, John Wayne type, he often couldn't bring himself to deal with problem employees.

Consequently, the leaders for both RI and KE became self-protective and short-sighted. KE's leader was an accountant who fretted over the cost of pencils. RI's leader was a hard-drinking salesman who was willing to settle for whatever conditions the big oil companies wanted. They not only lacked vision, they were averse to change, with a protectionist mentality. As a result, the company failed to focus on satisfying what its customers valued, build needed capabilities and capture available opportunities.

When my father put me in charge of KE, he told me I had free rein to do whatever I thought was best, except selling it. Even with my limited experience (I had just turned 26), I could see that big changes were required. Fortunately, I was too eager and too naïve to be intimidated.

When my father put me in charge of Koch Engineering, I knew big changes were required.

Distillation trays are devices that separate liquids by differences in boiling points. Despite having a superior product, the FLEXITRAY® valve tray, KE had managed to turn this asset into a liability by being difficult to work with. Most of the large engineering and operating companies had sophisticated engineering departments with a policy of checking product designs, but KE's management refused to share our design calculations. Customers were also unhappy with our tendency to be late with deliveries, which extended the downtime at their plants. Many of those delays were because our systems were poor. The Wichita office used an old IBM punch-card process that was outdated even by 1960s standards. We were about six months behind in our bookkeeping and there had been no physical inventory of the plant for at least two years. In short, we were slowly dying of self-inflicted wounds.

Our engineering business serving Europe and the Middle East was in even worse shape; it was losing money. Its leaders had decided to protect our manufacturing know-how by contracting different tray components with multiple fabricators in various countries, so that none of our suppliers could have the manufacturing knowledge to compete with us. This costly and complex arrangement crippled our business overseas. In both Wichita and Europe, I could see that we had to do a much better and more efficient job of creating value for our customers *as they defined it*.

Koch Engineering had a great product, but lacked customer focus.

CUSTOMERS FIRST

On the plus side, all these problems provided a ready-made laboratory for experimenting with the principles I had been learning since coming to Wichita. One such principle was that a voluntary transaction will only occur when both parties believe it will make them better off — thereby creating mutual benefit. That sounds simple, but it's amazing how many businesses get the value equation backwards, focusing first on what's in it for the business. They fail to grasp the obvious: their starting point should be creating value for the customer.

To better serve Koch Engineering's customers, we became more open and improved both the service and reliability of our Wichita plant. We began providing detailed design information to customers who requested it. We updated our antiquated business systems. To improve our service and competitiveness in Europe, everything was consolidated — design, manufacturing, sales, and management — into an efficient new facility outside Bergamo, Italy. These straightforward changes began producing large improvements almost immediately, allowing us to better serve our customers.

> **The starting point for any business should be creating value for the customer.**

I wish I could say the same about some of my other bright ideas. There were plenty that didn't work. Yet, despite my many missteps, the overdue combination of much-needed changes quickly turned KE's business around. More and more customers came to prefer us, sales took off and we became profitable. It was a classic win-win. But instead of settling for that improvement, I began looking for ways to use our newly developed capabilities to capture other opportunities by creating value for customers. In short, I set out to create a virtuous cycle, although I was far from fully understanding that model back then.

I believed that by adding related products we could build a diversified process equipment business, giving our customers more and better products at better prices. The first step was hiring an entrepreneurial commercial development person experienced with these products. With his help, we added a full range of tower internals. Through the years of innovation and acquisitions that followed, we became the world leader in distillation equipment and services by creating more efficient devices and designs, and by giving superior service. Following those successes, we extended the virtuous cycle by moving into heat exchangers, membranes, combustion, engineering and construction, pollution control, and, much later, data analytics. Because these developments and acquisitions allowed us to benefit customers and many others, we were rewarded.

Our acquisition of Tulsa-based John Zink in 1989, combined with a robust R&D program, enabled us to become the world leader in process burners and flares. Among our innovations were low NO_x technology, flare gas recovery and, most recently, "smart" burners. These were all highly valued by our customers. Our acquisition of Glitsch in 1997 added to our distillation products and gave us superior process plant engineering and construction capabilities, which enabled us to build better quality plants more efficiently than competitors.

In each of these successes, we made the acquisition not only because we believed we had the capability to significantly improve the business, but because it had capabilities that would improve our existing businesses and open new opportunities.

My late brother David, a gifted engineer, was essential to extending this virtuous cycle. In the nearly 40 years that he led what we called the Chemical Technology Group, it increased in size 50-fold. David had a gift for understanding technology and how it could create value, enabling him to foster innovation and growth.

My brother David was essential to extending our first virtuous cycle.

To extend this virtuous cycle, in 2018, ChemTech made a controlling investment in Genesis Robotics and Motion Technologies. GRMT commercializes innovative electric motor, gearbox and actuation technologies. Its founders viewed us as a preferred partner because of our culture, business and operational capabilities, and our philosophy of mutual benefit. As a Koch company, GRMT is now able to accelerate its strategy of enabling safer, faster, and more collaborative robots. Beyond robotics, GRMT's offerings have broad applicability to industrial automation, electrical and mechanical drivetrains, and exoskeletons for medical and industrial uses.

What's easy to overlook in this story is how much Koch's engineering businesses have improved the world around us. Our ultra-low emission burners and vapor recovery systems are helping keep the world's air cleaner. Our separation solutions improve water quality and food purity. Our products are helping us and manufacturers around the world to not only meet but exceed environmental expectations.

> Because of mutual benefit, we view acquisitions as a two-way street.

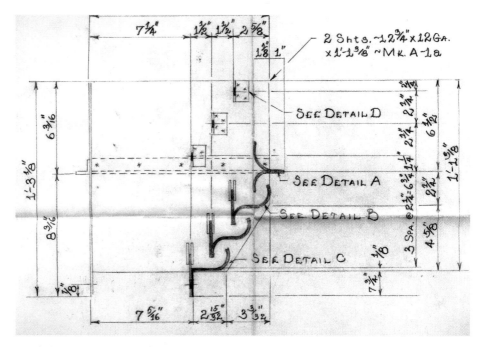

My father's 1949 drawing for our Kaskade tray. We gave up on this design after a customer accidentally installed it upside down and discovered it worked better that way.

Thanks to the creation of this virtuous cycle, one of our oldest and stodgiest businesses was utterly transformed. It is now bursting with ideas for a broader scope of value creation. Since 1961, ChemTech has grown more than 1,000-fold in revenue (and even more in net income) while benefitting the environment and enhancing worker safety worldwide. In 2019, the group's name was changed to Koch Engineered Solutions to reflect its transformative vision — one that calls for expanding its capabilities, entering new industries, improving knowledge sharing, increasing innovation, and building new and deeper preferred partnerships. I am confident KES will make it happen.

Koch's engineering businesses have improved
the world around us in many important ways.

KEY REFLECTIONS

1 What are the factors and attitudes that are holding me back from self-actualization? How can I overcome them?

2 Do I have a protectionist attitude toward new ideas and innovations? How do I become more open to improving myself in every way?

3 How can I apply the model of virtuous cycles to my own business, organization, or workplace?

The capabilities built for our gathering business opened the door for later businesses.

Gathering, Trading & Distribution

IN THIS SECTION

"...trial and error is a tremendously powerful process for solving problems in a complex world, while expert leadership is not."

– TIM HARFORD

ANOTHER EARLY VIRTUOUS CYCLE

After we began to turn around Koch Engineering, my father asked me to also help improve our crude oil gathering business, which generated a high percentage of our cash flow. As it turned out, we didn't just improve Rock Island. We transformed it, along with the national crude oil supply chain.

Like KE, RI was being held back by a protectionist mindset, but of a different sort. RI used small-diameter pipelines to transport crude from oil fields in southwest Oklahoma to a main line, where we sold most of the crude to major oil companies. The majors could be difficult to deal with, which was a big reason for our management's reluctance to expand out of the area. This left our modest piece of business, while profitable, essentially frozen. Fortunately, I found a kindred spirit in our Wichita office who was already beginning to break us out of that protectionist shell: Sterling Varner.

STERLING VARNER AS A ROLE MODEL

Sterling epitomized the self-actualizing person who creates his own internal virtuous cycle. He was born in an oilfield tent, suffered from lifelong health problems, stuttered, and never graduated from college. Yet he overcame all these obstacles to discover and develop his gifts and create tremendous value for the company, its customers, and everyone around him, including me. He was one of the most inspiring people I've ever known — the kind of person who could make countless contributions while making you feel like you contributed more.

Sterling had been working as a clerk for the Rock Island Oil & Refining Company in Duncan, Oklahoma, when our company acquired it in 1946. Several years later, my father brought Sterling to Wichita as a purchasing agent. Given Sterling's entrepreneurial passion, his role naturally grew. In 1969, he became vice president of Koch Industries, responsible for all our gathering, trading, and distribution businesses. Then, in 1974, he was named president and COO of Koch Industries, a position he held until his retirement in 1987. He was so dedicated to the company that he stayed on the board until his death in 2009. Everywhere he worked, he was instrumental in building the capabilities needed to create a virtuous cycle.

Sterling Varner (L) shared my passion for developing our capabilities.

A key to building our crude oil business was his knowledge of the business and the many relationships he established. He not only became liked and trusted throughout the industry, he had a vision for growth. He explained one of the first steps this way: "We were looking at different little pipeline systems, but when we bought Mohawk [a Tulsa-based crude oil trucking company], that was the first time we got into trucking." That simple statement is more significant than it sounds, because RI's management had always preferred pipelines to trucking. This really was a seismic development in the company history and an early sign of our focus on capabilities rather than specific industries. (More on that in the next Section.)

We also began adding other capabilities that our customers — the independent exploration companies — valued. When the majors changed their focus to looking offshore and overseas for bigger fields, they created an opportunity for us to greatly expand in crude oil gathering. Trucking became a critical capability, because it enabled us to be the first to gather oil in a new field. We had already proven we were much more efficient than the majors at building and operating pipelines; now we were demonstrating that we could give superior service in trucking. This gave us the courage to buy trucking companies everywhere, opening opportunities in virtually every oil field in the U.S. and Canada. Another capability we built was an outstanding sales team that helped create strong relationships with our customers and an understanding of what they valued.

During this transformation, we became devoted to becoming the preferred partner of our customers. If given a choice, most customers preferred moving their oil by pipeline, but our main competitors, the majors, typically required a reserve study and guarantees before building one. We, on the other hand, would build a pipeline just as soon as there was an indication the field was of sufficient size.

We began adding capabilities that our customers valued.

We also were able to move quicker by voluntarily buying pipeline rights-of-way, acquiring options on multiple routes rather than using the government's power of eminent domain. This enabled us to be the sole buyer of the oil and gave us the ability to assure our customers that we would always have a market for their oil. We made a point of being the quickest to pay for their oil and never bounced a check — two things of vital importance to cash-hungry explorers.

To ensure we could always move all the oil we gathered, we developed a trading capability. In those days, as Sterling recalled, "you could get all the crude oil you wanted, because it was just very difficult to sell it." That's why a trading capability was so important. "In the early days, oil was tough to market," agreed Bill Hougland, our most effective salesperson (and later the leader of the business). "One of the big things that helped us a lot was the fact that we never turned a lease back. We always found a way to market the oil."

With our reputation for superior service, prompt payments and a willingness to buy even in oversupplied markets, we succeeded in becoming the largest crude oil gatherer in the U.S. and Canada. At our peak we handled more than 1 million barrels per day, forming a critical part of the country's and the world's oil supply chain and benefiting tens of millions of people across the globe. That success was critical for creating an ongoing virtuous cycle based on our gathering, trading, and distribution capabilities.

These led to a similar opportunity in the gas liquids industry, which required many of the same capabilities. New natural gas discoveries in Kansas, Oklahoma, and Texas contained large amounts of liquids, so plants were being built to extract them. Our capabilities from crude oil supply enabled us to have similar success with gas liquids. When our volumes became sufficiently large, we built our own fractionation plant in Medford, Oklahoma, where we separated gas liquids streams into ethane, propane, and other products useful in society. This, in turn, provided the opportunity to build main lines for moving those products to markets on either the Gulf Coast or the Upper Midwest and trading them. The same became true for natural gas gathering, processing, trading, and distribution — furthering the virtuous cycle.

> We have utterly failed when we didn't follow the principles of MBM.

Then we acquired the primary pipeline for transporting ammonia from the Gulf Coast and distributing it throughout the Midwest. (Ammonia is made from natural gas and is the key ingredient in one of the three main plant nutrients, which makes it essential for the world's food supply.) Our next move — buying an ammonia plant in Louisiana to feed that pipeline system — was a failure, but it taught us what was important competitively. We used that insight to buy advantaged plants in the U.S., Canada, and Trinidad. These became a platform for trading and distributing fertilizers throughout the world.

Global trading 24/7 is now the norm for Koch companies.

The virtuous cycle didn't stop there. We then built capabilities to make our fertilizers more effective, developing products that improve fertilizer utilization. These advances enhanced the economics for farmers, boosting their crop yields while simultaneously benefitting the environment. People throughout the world depend on these products for their daily nutrition.

Our fertilizer business, which we named Koch Ag & Energy Solutions (KAES), was built by combining the capabilities of two virtuous cycles — gathering, trading and distribution, and the chemical process industries (described in the next Section). This combination opened new opportunities, such as methanol and phosphate production and distribution. The resources that this business produces, distributes, and trades are vital, not only to the world's food supply, but to a host of other life-enhancing products.

A critical development in getting KAES on the virtuous cycle track came in 2014, when we recognized the need to transform our flagship fertilizer plant in Enid, Oklahoma. At the time, its product mix was heavily slanted toward ammonia rather than UAN and urea (ammonia derivatives). This was a problem because ammonia was losing market share and becoming increasingly expensive to transport. To correct this and other deficiencies, and make Enid a world-class facility, we embarked on a $1.3 billion capital improvement project — the largest in Koch's history. Thanks to that investment, the plant is now highly competitive with an optimum product mix, efficient logistics, and a much better environmental footprint.

We don't have a monopoly on value creation.

We have succeeded in agriculture when we followed the principles of MBM and virtuous cycles, and utterly failed when we didn't. (As I mentioned in Section 2, much of the blame is mine. Faced with existential external threats, during this period, I failed to effectively apply our framework.) Some of our more punishing failures involved grain milling and trading, feed lots, meat processing, shelf-stable pizza crusts, animal feed and — most notably — Purina Mills. These misfires laid bare our inadequate capabilities and highlighted the consequences of not applying MBM, lessons that we have worked hard to learn from.

I wish I could say that agriculture was our only business with notable failures, but we made many of the same mistakes with tankers, coal, platinum trading, propane retailing, drilling rigs, and telecommunications — and for similar reasons. Many of our people were just using the language of MBM rather than truly applying it. Consequently, we failed to deliver the necessary benefit to our constituencies, which forced sometimes painful exits from various businesses and initiatives.

WHEN — AND WHY — TO SELL A BUSINESS

It's important to note that we have exited not only failed businesses but successful ones which no longer contributed to a virtuous cycle. Remember that crude oil gathering business we worked so hard to build? We spent four decades growing Koch Oil into one of our best and earliest success stories. But we sold it in 1999 as the business declined, and we probably should have sold it sooner. We also sell businesses that someone else values more, either because they have superior capabilities or a different point of view. We don't have a monopoly on value creation, so we need the humility to recognize when someone else can create greater value from an asset or business than we can.

The year we sold Koch Oil was also the year we created and were the first to offer weather derivatives, a popular product which traded on the Chicago Mercantile Exchange. These instruments gave investors a hedge against weather risk, which is a very important factor for utilities and large farming operations. We exited that market when insurance companies entered it, because they had better capabilities. We also sold our highly successful gas liquids business in 2005 because we mistakenly believed that natural gas production would continue to decline, limiting its future. (The subsequent invention of new fracking technology proved otherwise.) These mistakes are reminders of the importance of humility and continually improving our decision making.

> Our Vision requires us to continually revolutionize the way we create value.

All our businesses are continually transforming — especially with the help of new technology.

41

In 1998, Paul Wheeler, our head of corporate HR, sent a message to all employees explaining our decision to sell Koch Oil. His words demonstrate how consistent we have been in creating virtuous cycles of mutual benefit. "Our Vision," Wheeler wrote, "requires us to continually revolutionize the way we create value for our customers. Our Vision also requires us to identify business opportunities that best leverage and extend our knowledge and capabilities. To do this, every one of us must encourage and lead change." There can be no ongoing virtuous cycles of mutual benefit without the continual search for new vistas, for new opportunities to apply our capabilities to create superior value.

KEY REFLECTIONS

1 Why is trial and error important? Do I embrace it in my own life and work?

2 Am I applying my abilities to their fullest extent? Or am I focusing on areas and projects outside my abilities, on things that others could do better?

3 Is the end of a virtuous cycle a bad thing? What should I do when my progress seems stymied?

When Pine Bend Refinery opened in September 1955, it had a capacity of 25,000 barrels of crude per day. Today, refining, while greatly expanded, is just one of our many chemical process industries.

Chemical Process Industries

"Snowball effect:
a situation in
which something
increases in size
or importance
at a faster and
faster rate."

- CAMBRIDGE DICTIONARY

CREATING KOCH'S LARGEST CYCLE

In 1959, a former employee of my father's gave him the opportunity to purchase a one-third interest in Great Northern, the oil company that owned Pine Bend Refinery in Minnesota. My father took that opportunity and paid book value for the shares without even visiting the refinery. Ten years later, I put together a deal with the help of J. Howard Marshall II to acquire the remaining shares of Great Northern. That acquisition was arguably the most important in the history of Koch Industries. It gave us the capability to create a mutually beneficial cycle in a new arena: the chemical process industries.

My introduction to Pine Bend came in 1962 when my father sent me there for a six-month stint as a process engineer and, for a short time, salesman. (This assignment came after my time working with Koch Engineering and before I teamed up with Sterling to help him transform our crude oil business.) My diagnosis of Great Northern was that it, too, had the protectionist disease.

It was profitable because of a favorable market for Pine Bend's products and its advantaged crude supply, not because of its leadership. Like so many who confuse brains with a bull market, the management there thought they were the best at nearly everything. They certainly weren't interested in outside opinions. No wonder, then, that both the leaders and employees at Pine Bend vehemently resisted any transformation.

My last few weeks at Great Northern, working out of the sales office in Minneapolis, only confirmed its leadership and cultural deficiencies. In that office, they were little more than order takers who made no effort to identify new market needs, create value for customers, or even optimize output. The highlight of their day was a lengthy two-martini lunch (with or without a customer) at a fancy restaurant, after which they would spend most of the afternoon in their offices with the door closed.

THE IMPORTANCE OF CULTURE

Our vision for Pine Bend went beyond making major investments to improve and expand its capacity. We needed to transform the culture of the organization as well. But when we tried to do that, the response was a bitter, nine-month-long strike that led to violence and sabotage that could have resulted in fatalities. The conflict at Pine Bend showed how far people with a protectionist mindset are willing to go, even when change would benefit them. Entire companies and millions of jobs have evaporated because of similar attitudes, to say nothing of the decline of nations. Such are the consequences of abandoning mutual benefit.

Our champion for change at Pine Bend was Bernie Paulson, the new plant manager we brought in. Bernie was fearless in driving what needed to be done, regardless of opposition. He also had a knack for walking through a refinery asking questions of everyone, giving him ideas for improvements. Over time, that kind of hands-on, no-nonsense approach earned the respect of our employees there. And by applying our philosophy of mutual benefit, we eventually developed a very good relationship with the union.

Today's leadership team at Pine Bend runs one of the most energy-efficient refineries in the world.

As a result, Pine Bend has not only greatly improved its operations but its safety and environmental performance as well. For instance, Pine Bend has lowered criteria emissions by more than 70%, earned the EPA's ENERGY STAR® plant certification and a National Habitat Conservation award. It was the first refinery in the region to introduce ultra-low sulfur gasoline — years before the federal government mandated such products.

Our vision went beyond investments, improvements, and expansion. We needed to transform the culture as well.

We also recognized that we needed to transform sales at Great Northern every bit as much as operations, so we persuaded Joe Moeller to move from GN's service station business to quickly learn that capability. He soon led it and, reporting to Sterling Varner, transformed the business from being protectionist to being entrepreneurial, constantly seeking better ways to serve customers to our mutual benefit.

When my father acquired our initial one-third interest in Great Northern Oil Company, the capacity of Pine Bend was about 35,000 barrels of crude per day. When we fully acquired the company, its capacity was up to 80,000 barrels per day. Today, it can process 360,000 barrels of feedstocks that are difficult for most refineries to handle — more than 14 times its original capacity. It not only processes enormous volumes more reliably, efficiently, and safely — it does so while better protecting the environment. Thanks to our current team, Pine Bend now has one of the lowest emissions rates in the industry.

The value of owning Great Northern is hard to overestimate. Milton Hall, our former controller, put it this way: "That acquisition in 1969 was the key event in the history of Koch Industries, because it transitioned us from essentially being a pipeline and trucking company. It got us into the production of products that we had not really been directly involved with. So it opened many, many doors for growth and acquisitions." In other words, a virtuous cycle.

CAPABILITY- VS. INDUSTRY-FOCUSED

As with other virtuous cycles, this one was never dependent on a specific industry. Whereas many companies focus primarily on industries, Koch is focused on its capabilities. We have always been willing to enter industries if we feel we have the knowledge and expertise to create superior value. As I said earlier, we are not a conglomerate. Unlike conglomerates, we create superior value by combining the capabilities of our diverse businesses across many industries. Our capability-driven approach opens doors that would otherwise be shut or out of sight for an industry-focused company. What happened after our transformation of Pine Bend illustrates the difference.

By applying the capabilities we had developed in trading and distribution, we were able to optimize sales and distribution of the refinery's products. Pine Bend, in turn, eventually provided the genesis for many of our trading and distribution businesses in other industries. These included our asphalt business, Koch Materials. By growing its capabilities, we succeeded in developing the technology to make better roads and became the largest provider of asphalt emulsions in the nation.

> **Virtuous cycles are never dependent on a specific industry.**

Pine Bend also helped us launch Koch Minerals, which trades and distributes petroleum coke and other byproducts of refining. These are used as fuel sources, in electrical products, and other applications. Throughout all this growth and transformation, we continued to reinvest 90% of our profits, enhancing our ability to extend this new virtuous cycle.

In 1981, we used the capabilities we had built at Pine Bend to acquire and improve a refinery and chemicals complex in Corpus Christi, Texas. We closed that deal on a Friday the 13th, and for a few months afterward, everything about it seemed jinxed. Markets fell and demand was depressed. The hangover from the runaway inflation of the late 1970s was still a drag on the U.S. economy. But, by applying the capabilities we had built at Pine Bend, we began seeing improvements.

We eventually took the refining capacity in Corpus Christi from 55,000 to 350,000 barrels per day, greatly increased chemical production, built gathering and distribution networks, and improved the business in every other way. Our actions have provided concrete benefits for customers, suppliers, communities, and others, who have rewarded us accordingly.

The virtuous cycle we created with Pine Bend and Corpus Christi enabled KII to enter industries that no one had foreseen. Our success in transforming Corpus Christi led to the joint purchase of Hoechst's polyester business in 1999 and the acquisition of INVISTA from DuPont in 2004. (At the time, INVISTA was our largest acquisition ever.) By combining those two businesses, we created one of the largest polymer and fiber companies anywhere. INVISTA provided the nylon 6,6 fiber for almost half of all the automotive air bags made in the world. Its premium spandex fiber was a big hit with athletic apparel companies.

Since 2012, EPA publicly available data has ranked Koch Industries as either number one or number two in pollution reduction initiatives.

Despite owning popular fiber brands such as LYCRA® and STAINMASTER®, we realized that getting INVISTA into a virtuous cycle mode would be a long slog. During due diligence, we found material gaps in all five dimensions of our management framework. Many of INVISTA's businesses and assets were uncompetitive and saddled with an entitlement culture. Its poor information systems and measures made good decisions almost impossible. INVISTA also suffered from poor economic thinking and lacked beneficial incentives. Unfortunately, we made many of those problems worse by initially failing to apply the basics of MBM ourselves.

To correct this situation, Jeff Gentry moved from Koch Minerals to INVISTA in 2007. After finding the culture was still top-down and bureaucratic, with MBM only given lip service, he quickly replaced half of the leadership team. Many facilities were uncompetitive, causing the company to be unprofitable, so he immediately began restructuring the business by selling or shutting down disadvantaged assets. The one bright spot involved commercializing new ADN technology at INVISTA's Orange, Texas, facility. That change exceeded expectations.

We want everyone, everywhere, to have the opportunity to self-actualize.

These efforts allowed more employees to realize their potential, which got INVISTA on a better trajectory. In 2015, INVISTA began to take its transformation efforts to another level by eliminating waste even more aggressively. It built world-class plants in China, upgraded its remaining plants and installed a Business Process Transformation system that provides much better transparency throughout the value chain. Jeff and his team then focused on more fully empowering our employees to innovate and create added value for our customers. They sold the LYCRA® spandex business at a premium as its quality advantage became threatened.

Our capabilities, when applied to new businesses and opportunities, can create superior value.

We continued to add other chemical process industries to this cycle. The same year we bought INVISTA we acquired two wood pulp mills from Georgia-Pacific. Success with these led us to acquire all of GP the following year for $21 billion (about five times what we paid for INVISTA). Georgia-Pacific introduced us to the manufacture of tissue, paper, packaging, building products, and a shelfful of popular consumer products. Although GP was in better shape than INVISTA, it still fell short on all five dimensions of MBM.

We began addressing those deficiencies by changing GP's vision from a short-term to a long-term focus, and from being a low-cost upgrader of southern pine with no innovation, to continually innovating in ways that create superior value for customers. We also worked to create a challenge culture, improve measures and economic thinking, and completely overhaul its compensation system. We scrapped its hierarchical culture in favor of one that empowers employees (enabling self-actualization) and truly puts safety first. At GP and every part of Koch Industries, we are constantly striving to improve safety performance with a goal of zero incidents. More than 100 of our facilities have received outstanding safety awards and certifications. This is a source of pride and a spur to ensure that every workplace — especially those with unique risks — is as safe as possible.

> **We are constantly striving to improve safety performance with a goal of zero incidents.**

Georgia-Pacific served as a powerful reminder that one of the most difficult changes for us all is to change the way we think. To help drive that sort of transformation, Joe Moeller moved to Atlanta to become GP's CEO. What he found was the tale of two cities, caused by a feudal organizational structure in which upper management were self-serving protectionists while the great majority of the employees were dedicated and hard-working. It didn't take long for Joe to remove almost all the top layers of management, typically replacing them with entrepreneurial employees already in the organization.

His culture-changing efforts didn't stop there. Joe turned the 51st floor — which had been occupied by senior management and available to other employees by invitation only — into conference rooms open to all. He made a point of meeting and eating regularly with employees, solicited challenge, and generally signaled that every employee was respected and valued. With more than 300 manufacturing sites, these changes took time, but now GP has transformed itself in many ways, and is continuing to improve.

Another important acquisition in a different chemical process industry was Guardian Industries. Guardian is a leading maker of high-performance glass for buildings, such as the glass on the Freedom Tower in New York City and the structural skin of the world's tallest building in Dubai. Its SRG Global business makes innovative parts for vehicles, including chrome-plated grilles for some of the world's best-selling trucks. We are applying what we have learned from our other transformations to help Guardian do the same.

Few people — including some of our own employees, sometimes — realize how much these process industries have contributed to well-being in the world. Think of the lives saved because of our seatbelt and air bag fibers. Think of the improvements in public health thanks to our development of hands-free dispensers for paper towels, napkins, and eating utensils. Our glass products for the construction industry have improved appearances while reducing energy use. Every paper or wood product we produce begins with forest products sourced from suppliers with a proven commitment to sustainable practices.

Koch Engineered Solutions has a tremendous history of supplying innovative products and services to chemical process industries.

My rapid-fire retelling of these important developments doesn't begin to do justice to all the creative work of the dedicated employees who helped make those transformations a reality. What's important to see in this decades-long sequence of events is the consistent thread of how our capabilities, when applied to new businesses and opportunities, can create new value. Each example shows the need for new capabilities, which, in turn, will lead to new opportunities. These cycles can be continued indefinitely if we faithfully and fully apply our MBM framework to achieve self-actualization in our own lives.

KEY REFLECTIONS

1. Why does being capability focused lead to better results than being industry focused? How can I apply this concept personally?

2. Do I enhance or harm my company's culture?

3. How do MBM and its Guiding Principles bring about a beneficial culture?

Growth in Koch's Investment Portfolio

$40B

$0

1990   2020

With a presence in 60 countries, the financial complexities of Koch's businesses have grown exponentially.

Investments

"Every success story is a tale of constant adaptation, revision and change. A company that stands still will soon be forgotten."

– RICHARD BRANSON

THE IMPORTANCE OF REINVESTMENT

Companies have three ways to generate capital: issue equity, borrow money or generate earnings which are reinvested. At Koch, we reinvest 90% of our earnings. As a result, we have generated the capital needed for our growth without going public or taking on debt that would limit our flexibility.

THE BENEFITS OF BEING PRIVATE

We've preferred to grow by absorbing other types of risk as opposed to the risks that come with elevated leverage. Further, as a private company, we rely on our strong credit rating to help create lasting partnerships with customers and suppliers.

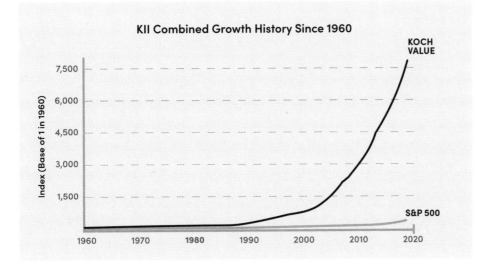

Koch Industries has outperformed the S&P 500 by a factor of 30-to-1 since 1960.

As a result, we typically have excess liquidity — sometimes significantly so — which provides opportunities to invest in new businesses. As our financial assets grew, it became critically important to have a strong investment capability — one that is flexible, since the nature and timing of future opportunities are unknowable.

Prior to 2005, our investments were largely limited to municipal bonds and municipal leasing. The municipal lending background of our investment team caused us to think too narrowly about our capabilities and miss opportunities.

That changed in a big way when we used our excess liquidity and debt to acquire Georgia-Pacific at the end of 2005. We were intent on retiring its debt and regaining our liquidity as quickly as possible, but we also needed to build a broad investment capability. The acquisitions of GP and INVISTA made us fiduciaries for large pension plans that had invested heavily in equities to optimize returns, which, in our minds, created excessive risk concentration.

To better diversify risk, we wanted to consider all asset classes and opportunities. So, we began to build investment teams to give us broader capabilities. This led to selling our municipal business and a focus on building a comprehensive investment capability: Koch Asset Management.

This group was able to manage all the relevant risks, including currency, liquidity, market, commercial and credit, and the perverse incentives usually found in structured financial instruments. Over the years, we have significantly expanded our capabilities, adding fixed income, trading, futures, and real estate. All our investment relationships are now based on our philosophy of mutual benefit, providing positive results for everyone involved — from our counterparties to the broader society.

The Atlanta skyline, with Georgia-Pacific's headquarters on the far right. Acquiring GP and INVISTA meant we needed a broader investment capability.

By 2010, KII's liquidity had started to rebuild, so we added capability in treasury as well. The approach was different because Koch Industries needed to adjust quickly as opportunities arose. (Pension requirements are much longer term.) Our treasury uses a somewhat similar risk framework, but the asset classes and related knowledge networks are quite different.

By 2013, interest rates were near historic lows, causing the returns on our portfolios to decline while driving acquisition valuations to unattractive levels. When others continued to make acquisitions at these inflated prices — without the capability to fully fund them — it created attractive investment opportunities for us in debt and preferred equity. We formed Koch Equity Development with a vision unlike most capital providers. Rather than locking into a set approach, KED provides whatever structure our counterparties want. All we require is that we be compensated for the risk and term.

This application of our mutual benefit philosophy has far exceeded my expectations. KED's first deal was a preferred investment that enabled the Weiss family to take American Greetings private. They told us after the deal closed that they had interviewed more than 30 potential

> All our investment relationships are based on mutual benefit.

partners, but we were the only one that fully listened to their needs. This was the first step in establishing KED's brand of mutual benefit that has made it a preferred capital provider. In fact, it was the Weiss family's recommendation that caused INSIGHTEC to come to Koch for capital. (See Section 6.) To date, KED has invested more than $12 billion with very good results for both us and our counterparties. The companies we invest in come out stronger, with a brighter future built on value creation. They win, and so do we.

As our liquidity grew, we continued to add capabilities, including the creation of Koch Real Estate in 2016. Knowing that real estate is the largest asset class in the world, our experience with Koch Asset Management following the 2008 financial crisis gave us the confidence to enter this business on the belief that we could offer added value to real estate developers and operators.

We have participated in the construction or redevelopment of more than 15 million square feet of office, warehouse, retail, and residential space across the U.S. and Europe. We've also partnered in more than 500 medical office, senior living and student housing projects, and nearly 100 marinas. Our opportunities grew as we added value for developers, causing them to see us as more than just a reliable source of capital. We also have knowledge of building products, an ability to evaluate and manage large projects, and a philosophy of mutual benefit.

OUR UNIQUE INVESTMENT VISION

Investing offers a unique way to benefit society.

Some of our most recent investment-related innovations have been built on long-standing, mutually beneficial relationships. For example, our partnership with Neuberger Berman has grown into a lending business that fills a need that banks and most private lenders can't address. Our partnership with Kayne Anderson has led to significant opportunities to fund various real estate and private credit opportunities. Our investment banking relationship with KeyBank in Cleveland has provided many benefits, including sourcing unique opportunities. Throughout these developments, our focus has been on becoming a preferred partner that can drive the expansion of this virtuous cycle in investments.

A $1,000 investment in Koch in 1960 would be worth $10 million today.

Investing offers a unique, if seldom understood, way to improve society. When capital is allocated to its highest-valued use, it leads to more innovation, more job opportunities, stronger and more resilient communities, and an overall higher standard of living. While our investment capabilities have grown tremendously, our focus on using them to create value has remained the same. We have no intention of letting that change.

Whether we're talking about finances, furnaces, forest products, fibers, or fuels, it should be obvious by now that a principled approach to business — one that relies on continual improvement and a commitment to mutual benefit — is essential for long-term success. This is especially true as we enter what could be the biggest virtuous cycle of all: using technology to improve people's lives.

KEY REFLECTIONS

1. Would you rather work for a company with lots of debt or lots of equity? Why?

2. How is Koch's view of risk different? How does that view shape your own?

3. How are you investing in yourself to improve your own capabilities and increase your contributions?

Manual typewriters, rotary-dial phones, and carbon paper used to be state-of-the-art office tools. The computer revolution changed all that — and even more dramatic changes are on the way.

———

Electronic & Data Technology

"... novel technologies arise by combination of existing technologies and therefore existing technologies beget further technologies ... we can say that technology creates itself out of itself."

— W. BRIAN ARTHUR

TECHNOLOGY GUIDED BY MBM

Tradition and nostalgia have their limits. In 1935, the year I was born, Northern proudly advertised a new bath tissue that was "soft and 100% splinter free." Can you imagine what toilet paper must have been like before then? I can, because the paper in our outhouse at the line camp where I worked at our Beaverhead Ranch was definitely not splinter free.

In recent years, software and electronic technologies have ushered in a new era of creative destruction for almost every industry. I believe this new era is likely to be KII's most promising yet, because these new tools greatly benefit *all* our businesses — including GP and the way it makes bath tissue. Tech is a strong enabler of our twin philosophies of mutual benefit and continual transformation. The individuals and companies that embrace it will greatly enhance their ability to help people improve their lives.

About 10 years ago, we recognized that information technology was transforming industry after industry and would soon transform all of ours. The conclusion was obvious: We needed to embrace the tech revolution and the creative destruction it entails. So far, we have invested more than $26 billion in technology in the last six years, creating a fifth virtuous cycle and enhancing our previous cycles.

Our first major technology-related acquisition was Molex in 2013. Molex had a long history of providing reliable and innovative electrical connectors for everything from smartphones to washing machines. We bought Molex because we believed it fit our philosophy of mutual benefit. We were confident we could help make it much more successful and that it could do the same for our businesses. To help Molex improve, we applied the five dimensions of MBM, starting with Vision. This ensured that its Vision more fully reflected changes in the global electronic marketplace. By 2020, Molex's Vision was focused on making a connected world possible by enabling the

technology that is transforming the future and improving people's lives. This Vision has greatly increased the company's opportunities.

A prime example is Molex's 5G automotive system that combines antennas with an electronic connectivity device. This system was recognized by Autonomous Vehicle Technology magazine with the 2020 ACES award. Unlike older, non-integrated offerings, Molex found ways to provide ultra-high data transmission by integrating multiple antennas. These high-speed data links are essential for connected and autonomous vehicles. For complex solutions beyond its capabilities, Molex partners with other suppliers to better provide differentiated value for its customers, some of whom are the biggest automotive manufacturers in the world.

Now that Molex is a Koch company, it has far greater access to capital as well as knowledge networks. It is using these advantages to acquire the capabilities needed to build integrated systems in several fields, including health care. Phillips-Medisize (acquired by Molex in 2016) partnered with a leading pharma company to develop the first FDA-approved caregiver-connected health device and ecosystem for automated drug delivery to the patient. Phillips-Medisize has since developed an even broader end-to-end connected health capability. It leverages proprietary drug-delivery technology built on Molex electronics and a cloud data platform provided by Koch Business Solutions.

Molex now embodies one of our Guiding Principles: Knowledge.

Molex is networking with several Koch companies — including Flint Hills Resources, Georgia-Pacific, INVISTA, and Koch Engineered Solutions — to develop technology that can provide timely, analytics-driven insights regarding gas leaks, corrosion, heat and vibration. Molex is experimenting with Guardian's SRG Global on ways to incorporate

electronic assemblies or embed sensors into plastic and then jointly sell those products. Molex now embodies one of our Guiding Principles (Knowledge, which calls for acquiring and proactively sharing best practices) by furthering the education of all our businesses when it comes to relevant technology trends.

A subsequent and even bigger tech investment was the acquisition of Infor, which creates easy-to-use business cloud software that is specialized by industry. Koch companies have worked in mutually beneficial relationships with Infor ever since our initial investment in 2017. One of the

Automotive content management systems developed by Molex are powering the future of connected vehicles.

best examples of this was Infor's creation of an enterprisewide tool called myHR. Now, for the first time, our human resources organization has a truly global technology solution that provides easy access to employee information — regardless of where someone works or for which business.

Even better, Infor's myHR tool is making it easier for Koch employees to self-actualize. Walt Malone, our head of corporate HR, explains it this way: "If you're an employee asking yourself, 'Where is my best opportunity?' or 'What role am I best suited for?' — or if you're a supervisor wondering, 'Where am I going to find someone who's really good at the new role we're creating?,' this tool helps provide the answers much more efficiently and effectively."

Infor has invested about $4 billion in product design and development to deliver industry-specific CloudSuites that solve the most challenging operational issues for more than 68,000 customers worldwide. Infor's CloudSuites are cloud-native, industry-specific tools that help companies modernize and drive immediate, tangible improvement. Infor's key industries include manufacturing, distribution, healthcare, public sector, retail, and hospitality.

Jim Hannan, who helped lead this acquisition, views it as both transformative and mutually beneficial. "Software is no longer an industry vertical; it is a disruptive layer that is transforming every facet of society. As a global organization spanning multiple industries across 60 countries, Koch has the resources, knowledge, and relationships to help Infor continue to expand its transformative capabilities."

Among our other tech-related acquisitions are i360, which excels at data aggregation and analysis, and EFT Analytics, which uses predictive analytics to improve the reliability and efficiency of manufacturing processes.

THE BENEFITS OF DISRUPTIVE TECHNOLOGY

An important broad initiative to increase our access to technologies and ideas that can enhance our virtuous cycles was the formation of Koch Disruptive Technologies in 2017. KDT, which is led by my son, Chase, is all about creative destruction. It originates and invests in promising entrepreneurs and technologies to improve

and transform Koch's existing businesses and create new technology platforms and other opportunities for the company. It is also expanding our knowledge networks, and not just in Silicon Valley. We have found that some of the most promising disruptive technology is being developed far from the usual tech hotspots.

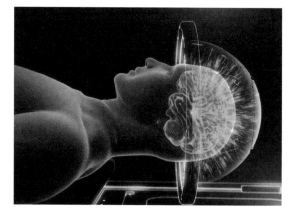

INSIGHTEC's surgery- and drug-free treatment for essential tremor is creating new hope for millions.

KDT's first opportunity was a company called INSIGHTEC, based in Israel, which developed disruptive medical technology. INSIGHTEC discovered a new way to target and treat damaged or diseased brain tissue — including the kind that causes uncontrollable tremors — using focused ultrasound instead of a scalpel or medications. Results are immediate, with no need for lengthy recovery from highly invasive surgery. INSIGHTEC had already received FDA approval for treating essential tremor but needed additional capital and other capabilities to address many other neurological disorders and expand globally.

In the past six years, Koch has invested more than $26 billion in technology.

Despite its tremendous prospects, INSIGHTEC was losing money. KDT helped by initially investing $100 million of much-needed capital, and significantly more since. In addition, KDT showed how to use MBM to improve certain aspects of INSIGHTEC's business. We have also helped demonstrate the benefits of its technology to regulatory agencies. INSIGHTEC has enormous potential to make a dramatic difference in the lives of those afflicted with brain disorders. If successful, this new technology could be used to help millions of people around the world. The potential benefit is enormous.

Another KDT investment was Denver-based Ibotta, the leading mobile rewards app in the U.S. Ibotta offers cash-back rewards on purchases of groceries, clothing, travel, and many popular consumer products. Shoppers can earn additional rewards by paying through the Ibotta app. As Chase noted, "Ibotta is a key player in the $100 trillion global payments market." We believe the upside for Ibotta is tremendous — far beyond the 35 million consumers that have downloaded the app — including great potential for GP's consumer business.

INSIGHTEC and Ibotta illustrate the unique and very important role that Koch Disruptive Technologies has in our technology cycle of mutual benefit. KDT serves a special purpose, because it is the one Koch company solely focused on truly disruptive technologies — high-potential ideas capable of replacing current alternatives. It is funneling new platforms to Koch that offer multiple ways to create new value. As with

Molex, KDT's success depends on the philosophy of mutual benefit. It does more than provide capital to breakthrough companies; it brings them significant value through our MBM framework and the opportunity to leverage Koch capabilities.

KOCH LABS

Also central to KDT's vision is investing in companies whose technology will improve one or more of our businesses. When we can help an innovator prove or demonstrate a technology, it often makes us the preferred investor. We call this strategy Koch Labs. A prime example is KDT's investment in Outrider, which developed autonomous vehicles for positioning trucks in shipping-and-receiving yards. KDT learned of this opportunity through GP, which was experimenting with Outrider's system. While many companies would consider the prospect of technology disrupting a core business as a threat, Koch proactively embraces technology-driven change. Why? Because it enables us to succeed by making a bigger contribution.

> **KDT invests in technology companies that will be mutually beneficial.**

Technology acquisitions and investments such as these are helping our industrial businesses transform themselves, while simultaneously being transformed by our MBM framework. As we share knowledge back and forth across Koch, our own businesses serve as valuable laboratories for developing technology products and services.

As we've discussed, the mutual benefits from Koch's knowledge sharing range from life-changing medical advances to improved environmental stewardship and reductions in energy use. But everyday jobs can be transformed, too. Much of what used to be dull or dangerous work can now be handled by technological solutions. No more climbing 200-foot ladders wearing 50 pounds of safety gear to check a valve. Less risk of carpal tunnel syndrome from endless and mindless data input. Fewer frustrations or bad decisions because we don't have the right information. And an end to many of the surprises in the plant that used to arise from unexpected maintenance issues.

Just as important is the fact that these technological innovations can free employees to do higher-value work that is more challenging and rewarding. This gives employees more opportunity to transform their roles so they can self-actualize and create their own virtuous cycles.

I believe the era of digitally driven change has only just begun and is likely to be the most remarkable period in our existence. What follows in the next section are some amazing real-life examples of how we're putting this knowledge to work through the application of our Republic of Science model — examples that I hope will motivate and inspire you as you pursue your own transformation and that of your organization.

KEY REFLECTIONS

1. How do we use technology to benefit both individuals and society?

2. How can I use technology to help develop my abilities?

3. How do I prepare for technology-driven changes to my role?

In a true Republic of Science, every employee innovates, challenges, and shares knowledge.

Fostering A Republic of Science

"The biggest sources
of opportunity are
collaboration and
partnership."

- MARK PARKER, NIKE CHAIRMAN

THE REPUBLIC OF SCIENCE

The Republic of Science model — getting all our businesses to share knowledge and help each other for the benefit of Koch Industries as a whole — is central to virtuous cycles. It brings our capabilities into collision with each other, not in a violent way, but in a mutually reinforcing manner that enables us to double down on mutual benefit. The more we share knowledge and collaborate, the more innovations we employ and opportunities we seize, enabling us to greatly increase our ability to succeed by contributing to others.

A case in point was enabling Flint Hills Resources to greatly improve its ability to execute leak detection and repair. Finding and preventing leaks is a critical component of FHR's environmental program, but also a complex and high-risk challenge. Employees and contractors often deal with daunting physical challenges while performing required inspections. In 2015, FHR decided to investigate new ways of handling leak detection. The environmental team leading this effort recognized that the U.S. Environmental Protection Agency needed to be a preferred partner — especially when improving regulations or implementing new solutions. When the EPA agreed to collaborate, we jointly began drawing up research and development plans.

Simultaneously, FHR found that Molex was developing sensor technology that seemed ideal for meeting the challenge of improved leak detection. By working together, the two leveraged FHR's industrial experience with Molex's growing system capability.

In Koch, the EPA gained a partner with a range of capabilities that shortened the R&D cycle. Molex already had the necessary sensors, software, and analytics capabilities, and FHR understood where the pain points and waste were in existing procedures. Everyone realized that the opportunities for mutual benefit among the three parties were enormous. Finding the right solution could help facility operators in a wide variety of industries detect leaks quickly, thereby reducing emissions while enhancing compliance, reducing costs, and creating a safer workplace.

After a year of testing, the system was installed in two process units at one of FHR's refineries. Thanks to positive results, FHR is now developing further leak detection and risk reduction systems for other kinds of process units. Meanwhile, Molex has applied these innovations to create a new business focused on the industrial internet of things: Molex IIoT Solutions. It provides systems to improve plant utilization and safety, once again demonstrating our philosophy of mutual benefit in action.

Another example is Koch Engineered Solutions' new vision, which centers on adapting and utilizing knowledge throughout KII to create more value for KES's customers.

> We can all accomplish more when we cooperate and combine our strengths.

Two years ago, John Zink Hamworthy Combustion, the process combustion and pollution control business of KES, began collaborating with Flint Hills Resources to improve the efficiency of combustion systems. Both Flint Hills Resources and John Zink Hamworthy Combustion believed if they could get full operating data from FHR's furnaces and then run it through JZHC's engineering models, it would allow FHR to optimize its furnace performance. Fortunately, FHR had already created the necessary digital capability, which it combined with other tools to access the data.

Their solutions gave furnace operators real-time data for the first time. After applying the new technology to one furnace and running the data through JZHC, the operators saw immediate benefits in furnace performance, including fuel savings and increases in yields. This solution, which FHR helped JZHC develop, is called EMBER™, and is now part of a larger array of combustion optimization solutions. Thanks to this close collaboration, FHR has been able to rapidly install EMBER™ elsewhere and is planning to scale the solution to more than 140 furnaces across FHR.

For employees in operational roles, access to real-time data has been a game changer.

If test results continue to be positive, FHR will be able to save on fuel, increase yields, improve safety, and reduce emissions. Results from those installations will also give JZHC the kind of real-world data needed to help it sell its solution to non-Koch companies. Another KES company, EFT Analytics, which has extensive experience building custom software platforms for customers, is contributing to this effort. Widespread adoption will result in worldwide environmental benefits.

Other companies within KES are also developing "smart plant" value propositions along the lines of those at JZHC. One of those, called Tower View by Koch-Glitsch, has generated very promising test results for FHR. Koch Separation Solutions may also benefit from similar platforms. The combination of the capabilities that led to these offerings promotes increased visibility, speed to market, and greater value for customers.

COMPLEMENTARY CAPABILITIES

Paul Houslet, vice president of transformation for FHR, sums it up this way: "For me, projects like this are what distinguish virtuous cycles of mutual benefit between companies with complementary capabilities. Both companies bring to the table capabilities that the other doesn't and both are realizing benefits that they probably wouldn't have on their own. The results of our work are serving as a foundation for continued innovation and value creation as FHR transforms its plant operations and as JZHC transforms its business model and grows its new Smart Combustion business." His emphasis on complementary capabilities is spot-on: Individuals and organizations can accomplish more when they cooperate and combine their strengths, thereby overcoming weaknesses and identifying new opportunities.

Tom Korb, JZHC's vice president of Smart Combustion, agrees: "EMBER™ has been the most effective collaboration I have experienced in my career. If we can inspire this same level of collaboration across the company, the results will be staggering."

Happily, dozens of similar examples of innovation and transformation can now be found across Koch, which bodes well for our future. For example, after a remote monitoring capability developed by GP's Technology Group in Atlanta was successfully tested at the GP gypsum facility in Savannah, Georgia, the results were so encouraging — less unplanned downtime, more accurate monitoring — that the technology is now being developed for application at 140 other GP sites.

Another example is Molex's work with GP to develop an affordable sensor monitoring system that helps visualize vibration data remotely, regardless of what brand of sensors is being used. Validation of this product at a GP site gave Molex an important new product to sell to others and provided GP with a cost-effective alternative to expensive proprietary systems. These savings translate into lower prices for consumers and more investment and innovation at the company.

INVISTA provides additional examples. It has successfully developed next-generation technology for making ADN (a key ingredient for nylon 6,6 polymer) that eliminates benzene from the production process. This means employees now have a safer workplace and communities have a cleaner environment, while the company benefits from increased production and margins.

As mentioned earlier, INVISTA has also transformed the platform for its business processes. Instead of wrestling with three non-standardized and incompatible vendor products, it has given employees a single and more flexible platform that works globally. The new platform has streamlined and simplified processes, created greater transparency, lowered freight and logistics costs, and improved on-time deliveries. INVISTA has also improved its approach to using innovation to benefit customers and vendors, which has resulted in strategic, long-term licensing contracts that benefit both parties.

THE CHALLENGE PROCESS

Within a Republic of Science, challenge is essential. By this, I mean continual questioning and brainstorming to find a better way of doing things. It is an opportunity to learn and improve in a respectful environment, not a chance to shoot down another person's ideas. Given the importance of challenge, we have made it a key element of our culture. To ensure we have effective challenge, we include those with different perspectives, kinds of knowledge, and expertise. This

Within a Republic of Science, challenge is essential, but must be done respectfully.

kind of diversity is important for innovation and decision making, not only in the company but in society. Without challenge, there is little progress. And without progress, virtuous cycles of mutual benefit will not exist.

KEY REFLECTIONS

1 What is the Republic of Science, and why does it matter?

2 What knowledge do you have that could benefit others in the company?

3 Do you welcome challenges to your thinking and decisions?

Nearly a century ago, Charles deGanahl not only mentored my father, he gave him tremendous opportunities to grow and succeed. My father was so impressed with deGanahl that he named me after him. Mr. deGanahl has always been an inspiration to me because he was dedicated to creating virtuous cycles.

Charles deGanahl

Charles deGanahl Koch

As Simple as Possible, but No Simpler

IN THIS SECTION

Five Tips for Self-Actualization

"We can learn from self-actualizing people what the ideal attitude toward work might be under the most favorable circumstances ... the need for meaningful work, for responsibility, for creativeness, for being fair and just, for doing what is worthwhile and for preferring to do it well."

- ABRAHAM MASLOW

Above all else, this survey of virtuous cycles at Koch Industries proves one thing: Amazing things are possible when people self-actualize.

Everything can be improved.

None of our progress would have been possible without employees who discovered their innate abilities, developed them into valued skills, applied them to maximize their contributions, and then did it all over again. When individuals create these virtuous cycles at a personal level, they become engaged and develop meaning in their lives by continually taking their ability to learn, grow, and contribute to a higher level. That process has become an essential aspect of who we are as a company.

Yet what can be improved, must be improved. For Koch Industries to continue to create virtuous cycles of mutual benefit and succeed in this new world of rapid and fundamental change, we must do a better job of enabling our employees to create their own virtuous cycles. By becoming contribution motivated, they will not only enable the company to succeed, they will realize their potential and have much more successful, fulfilling lives.

Building the foundation for a happy and fulfilling life takes time and effort. No government, organization, friend, or family member can do the heavy lifting for you. If you are serious about pursuing a path of self-transformation and want to create or contribute to virtuous cycles of mutual benefit, here are some quick and easy reminders to help keep you on track:

① KNOW YOUR TRUE ABILITIES.

Constantly explore to discover your aptitudes — what you naturally do well — then pursue whatever you enjoy that will enable you to contribute. To succeed, we must be realistic about our abilities and where they can create value. Take note of how you spend (or waste) your time.

② WORK HARD TO DEVELOP YOUR ABILITIES.

You must master the application of your gift if you want to make the greatest possible contribution. At the age of 84, I'm still striving daily to enhance my abilities to create more value. Don't waste your life trying to succeed in a role you're not good at.

③ APPLY YOUR ABILITIES IN WAYS THAT BENEFIT OTHERS.

True success comes from benefitting others as the way to benefit yourself. As you encounter obstacles to self-actualizing and creating mutual benefit, don't give up — find the right occupation and then dedicate yourself to it. As Maslow warned: "If you deliberately plan to be less than you are capable of becoming, you'll be deeply unhappy the rest of your life."

④ CONTINUALLY TRANSFORM YOURSELF.

Continuous improvement is not a process, it's a way of life. No matter how much success you achieve, be dedicated to lifelong learning. Don't let success destroy your initiative or willingness to embrace change — and don't let failures cause you to give up. If you see something that is wrong or wasteful, even (or especially) if it's a policy from on high, challenge it. And, if at first you don't succeed, keep challenging.

My parents were both lifelong learners, and they raised me to be the same.

⑤ HAVE A PURPOSE IN LIFE.

What is your North Star? What guides your actions? The desire to make money, be popular, enjoy life's pleasures, or live as long as possible is not the same as a having a true purpose. I believe your greatest rewards will come from becoming contribution motivated in ways that draw on your gifts.

I wish you the very best in this journey, knowing full well that as you succeed, all those around you will be better off, too.

Charles G. Koch
Wichita, Kansas
Spring 2020

Guiding Principles

❶ INTEGRITY

Have the courage to always act with integrity.

❷ STEWARDSHIP & COMPLIANCE

Act with proper regard for the rights of others. Put safety first. Drive environmental excellence and comply with all laws and regulations. Stop, think and ask.

❸ PRINCIPLED ENTREPRENEURSHIP™

Practice a philosophy of mutual benefit. Create superior value for the company by doing so for our customers and society. Help make Koch the preferred partner of customers, employees, suppliers, communities and other important constituencies.

❹ TRANSFORMATION

Transform yourself and the company. Seek, develop and utilize the visions, strategies, methods and products that will enable us to create the greatest value.

5 KNOWLEDGE

Acquire the best knowledge from any and all sources that will enable you to improve your performance. Share your knowledge proactively. Provide and solicit challenge consistently and respectfully.

6 HUMILITY

Be humble, intellectually honest and deal with reality constructively. Develop an accurate sense of self-worth based on your strengths, limitations and contributions. Hold yourself and others accountable to these standards.

7 RESPECT

Treat everyone with honesty, dignity, respect and sensitivity. Embrace different perspectives, experiences, aptitudes, knowledge and skills in order to leverage the power of diversity.

8 SELF-ACTUALIZATION

Be a lifelong learner and realize your potential, which is essential for fulfillment. As you become increasingly self-actualized you will better deal with reality, face the unknown, creatively solve problems and help others succeed.